TRADITIONAL CHRISTMAS CRAFTS

TRADITIONAL CHRISTMAS CRAFTS

25 simple projects with step-by-step instructions

DEBORAH SCHNEEBELI-MORRELL

COLLINS & BROWN

DEDICATION
For my children Hannah and Rafi

First published in Great Britain in 1997
by Collins & Brown Limited
London House
Great Eastern Wharf
Parkgate Road
London SW11 4NQ

1 3 5 7 9 8 6 4 2

British Library Cataloguing-in-Publication Data:
A catalogue record for this book
is available from the British Library.

ISBN 1 85585 418 X (hardback edition)

ISBN 1 85585 419 8 (paperback edition)

Conceived, edited and designed by Collins & Brown Limited

Design conceived by Janet James
Editor: Gillian Haslam
Designer: Sara Kidd
Photography: Heini Schneebeli
Stylist: Deborah Schneebeli-Morrell

Reproduction by La Cromolito

Printed and bound in Germany by Mohndruck

AUTHOR'S ACKNOWLEDGEMENTS
Very special thanks to Heini Schneebeli for his care and attention to detail
in taking the really brilliant photographs in this book. And to my good
friends who have happily lent me beautiful objects as props and who have
allowed us to use their lovely homes in which to photograph some of the
projects – Raynes and Patrick Minns and Jill Patchett and Alan Du Monceau.
I would also like to thank Gloria Nicol for her constant encouragement
and useful advice and for making the lovely projects on pages 65, 73, 75 and 81.
Special thanks also to her mother, Alice Nicol, who interpreted and expertly made
the Christmas stockings on pages 90-95. Lastly, a big thank you to Maggie Colwell
who made the striking starbursts on page 37.

Contents

Introduction

IN THE NORTHERN hemisphere, the festival of Christmas takes place in deepest winter and at the darkest time of the year, around the winter solstice. We all yearn for snowfall to produce the much-loved fairytale white Christmas. In fact, in warmer climates, where real snow is unheard of, the curious artificial variety is extensively used to try to create a true wintry feel. However, there is no substitute for the real thing which brings a feeling of excitement and anticipation with it. Familiar traditions are essential to create a festive atmosphere – the bringing in of the tree from the forest on Christmas Eve and transforming it with sparkling decorations and a star, the guiding light of the three Magi. We make and display a circular wreath from living plants to represent the continuity of life and to herald the return of spring, we light log fires and candles to comfort and warm ourselves, and also to symbolize the welcome return of the sun.

It is a season when much more time is spent indoors, a time in which we feel able to give our creative ideas a focus, that of giving and receiving, preparing food for family and friends, baking and entertaining, and making cards, gifts, ornaments, tree and room decorations. Making your own decorations is a most rewarding activity, creating lasting presents, ornaments and mementoes which can become treasured additions to family collections passed down from generation to generation and brought out each year to delight and surprise.

Many of the beautiful and enchanting projects in this book are drawn from the rich folk traditions found in cultures where imaginative use is made of many different materials. Some projects are more contemporary in feel and make good use of modern materials. However, they all continue the theme of the transformation of easily available and inexpensive materials into wonderful and decorative objects which will give so much enjoyment and enhance and beautify your home at Christmas.

These star-shaped candle holders are made from papier mâché pulp. With a colored night light sitting snug in the center, they give out a warm and welcoming glow.

CHAPTER ONE

Golden Splendor

With the revival of interest in folk art and crafts from other cultures, working with metal foils is becoming more popular. It is a surprisingly easy and rewarding medium to use. No special skills or tools are necessary and simple techniques produce spectacular results.

Copper Placements

FOR A REALLY SPECIAL festive occasion, these beautiful, personalized copper name plaques are surprisingly easy to make. The lightweight soft copper foil is thin enough to cut with a small pair of embroidery scissors. A stunning and really professional effect can be produced with *repoussé* designs by working on the back of the metal foil with an old, dried up ball-point pen and a sewing tracing wheel.

Copper is such a soft metal that this simple drawing technique creates a raised design on the surface which catches the light beautifully. With age and exposure to air, the copper will tarnish, producing a subtle antique effect. However, it can be easily restored to its initial brightness with metal polish.

Why not make a special after-dinner gift of the name plaques for each guest as a glimmering memento of the evening. They could be used again, pinned to a bedroom or cupboard door or even fixed to the front of a very special notebook or photo album.

MATERIALS

FOR FOUR NAME PLAQUES

Tracing paper template

Copper foil 0.1 mm ($^4/_{1,000}$ in) thick, 160 x 20 cm (63 x 8 in)

Dry ballpoint pen

Small, sharp embroidery scissors

Wad of tissue paper

Sewing tracing wheel

Invisible tape

Tracing paper

Fine, black felt-tip pen

10

Copper Placements

1

Lay the template onto the copper foil and stick firmly in place with the tape. Carefully cut around the template with the small embroidery scissors.

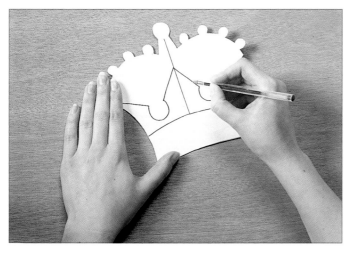

2

With the template still in place, draw lightly over the dark lines with the dry ball-point pen to transfer this part of the pattern onto the copper foil (this is now the back of the plaque).

3

Remove the template and place the copper face down on a wad of tissue paper or similar soft surface. Using the tracing wheel, draw the margin around the crown shape, the lines that were lightly marked through the template and the tramlines around the space for the name.

4

Fill in the dots and parallel lines and draw the stars into the bobbles at the top of the crown. Draw around a coin to make the circles and draw a star in the centers.

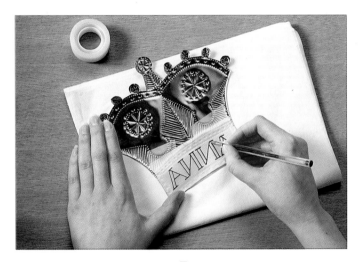

5

Lay a piece of tracing paper over the area at the base of the crown left blank for the name. With the black felt tip pen draw in your chosen name to fit the space. Remove the tracing paper, turn it back to front and with the ball-point pen draw over the letters, using some pressure to transfer them onto the back of the metal. Remove the tracing paper and finish working the letters freehand.

Enlarge this template on a photocopier to 200%. This template is also used for the project on page 18; the vertical lines in the lower part of the crown apply only to that project

13

Copper Candle Crowns

SOFT COPPER FOIL is one of the most rewarding metals to work with, its pliable surface yielding beautifully to the point of a bradawl, resulting in this pierced geometric design.

These glowing freestanding copper candle crowns can be used in a line along a festive dining table or in a group as a table centerpiece. If arranged on a reflective surface such as a copper or brass tray, they cast wonderful reflections in the shiny surface as well as projecting pinpricked patterns of light as the candle flame burns within.

When summer comes and thoughts of the cold, dark winter are forgotten, these crowns could be used to illuminate an outside evening meal. They are, of course, weatherproof, but may tarnish slightly, with the metal gaining a lovely warm, pinky glow.

MATERIALS

Roll of soft copper foil 0.1 mm ($^4/_{1,000}$ in) thick and 16.5 cm (6½ in) wide

Large scissors for cutting the copper

Chinagraph pencil

Ruler

Small pot lid as a template

Small, pointed scissors

Hole punch

Piece of cardboard

Bradawl

3 brass paper fasteners

Copper Candle Crowns

1

Cut a piece of the copper foil 25.5 cm (10 in) long by 16.5 cm (6½ in) wide. Draw on the pattern, as shown, using a chinagraph pencil. Simple geometric patterns are best but vary the design on each crown you make. Create the scalloped edge along the top of the copper foil by drawing around a pot lid as a template.

2

Using the small, pointed scissors, carefully cut around the marked lines of the scalloped edge. A small extra strip on the right edge of the copper has been left to tuck under and make a join when the copper is rolled into a cylinder.

3

Using the hole punch, make the large holes as shown in each scallop and along the straight edge of the base. Lay the copper onto the cardboard and evenly pierce holes with the bradawl, using the chinagraph lines as a guide. This will produce rough points of metal on the back, so do be careful when handling it.

4

When the piercing is complete, roll the copper loosely into a cylinder shape, tucking the extra strip inside at the join. Make three large holes with the bradawl through the two thicknesses of copper and insert the brass paper fasteners to hold the cylinder together, opening the arms out flat on the inside of the crown.

Copper Candle Sconce

M ANY PEOPLE WOULD NEVER dream that they possess the skills necessary to work with different metals. However, they are really very simple to learn. The method used is quite simple – no special techniques are required, and some everyday tools have been adapted, namely a dry ball-point pen and a sewer's tracing wheel.

Piercing and punching soft metal, like copper, is a well known folk art technique, and some of the best examples have become collectors' items. Here it is used to great effect on a grand theme. This crown pattern makes an interesting shape and is a perfect shield for the candle behind, with the glowing light radiating through the pierced holes and from behind, thus delineating the regal crown shape. These sconces have been designed to stand on a shelf or mantelpiece. For safety's sake, place the nightlights in small glass jars.

MATERIALS

Roll of soft copper foil 0.1 mm
($^4/_{1,000}$ in) thick and 16.5 cm
(6½ in) wide

Tracing paper template
(see page 13)

Invisible tape

Dry ballpoint pen

Small, pointed scissors

Piece of cardboard

Sewing tracing wheel

Bradawl

Hole punch

Aluminum can

Strong scissors

Protective gloves

3 brass paper fasteners

18

Copper Candle Sconce

1

Cut a piece of copper foil 20 x 16.5 cm (8 x 6½ in) and lay the tracing paper template on top. Stick in place with invisible tape and draw over the lines with the dry ball-point pen, pressing very lightly onto the foil beneath to transfer the outline and design. You will need to place the foil on a piece of cardboard or a pile of tissue paper – this provides a yielding surface and protects the worktop.

2

Remove the template to reveal the faint impression of the design. Use the small, pointed scissors to cut carefully around the outline, paying particular attention to the small bobbles along the top.

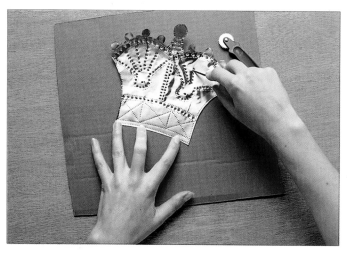

3

Place the crown shape on the cardboard or tissue. Roll the tracing wheel firmly over the transferred lines, add more decoration at this point if you like, then pierce through the copper from the front with the bradawl.

4

Next, using the hole punch, make the larger holes in the bobbles along the top of the crown. You will need to press the handles of the punch together very firmly to produce a neat hole with clean edges.

5
....

Cut down an aluminum can leaving 3.5 cm (1¼ in) upstanding from the base. This is easily done with strong scissors, but you may wish to wear gloves to protect your hands from any sharp edges. Wrap the copper crown around the aluminum can base and, using the bradawl, pierce three holes through both metals.

6
....

Push each paper fastener through these holes and open out the two arms behind the crown and inside the can, making sure they are pushed firmly back, allowing the crown to stand upright.

Leafy Aluminum Garland

THREAD THESE SPARKLING silvery oak leaves onto a silver cord and make a festive garland to drape around the beautiful blue glaucous needles of a Nordmann Christmas tree, hung with silver baubles. The addition of white fairy lights catches the reflective surface of the shiny metal, perhaps making us believe we are in the forest of the Ice Queen.

Aluminum is soft and the easiest to use of all the metal foils. It is reminiscent of all the marvellous tin work that appears in folk art throughout the world.

You may like to develop this project and create different varieties of leaves to thread alternately onto a garland. Make long garlands to drape across a room or weave them around a thicker wire circlet to create a shimmering metal wreath.

MATERIALS

Template

Roll of aluminum foil 16.5 cm (6½ in) wide and 0.1 mm (⁴⁄₁,₀₀₀ in) thick

Wad of folded tissue paper

Dry ballpoint pen

Sewing tracing wheel

Small, pointed scissors

Bradawl

2 m (2¼ yd) silver cord

Leafy Aluminum Garland

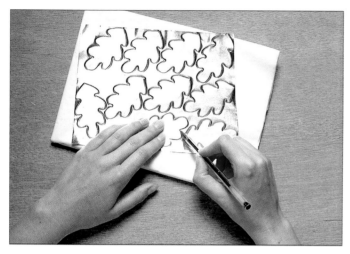

1

Place the template on the aluminum foil and rest it on the wad of tissue paper to make a yielding mat and to protect your work surface. Draw around the template carefully with the dry ball-point pen, pressing firmly. You will need to draw about 20 leaves.

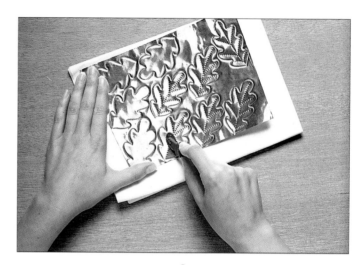

2

Remove the template. Pressing hard with the tracing wheel, make the pattern of the leaf veins on the aluminum foil. Carefully cut out each leaf with the small, pointed scissors about 2 mm (⅛ in) away from the outline of the leaf.

Trace over this leaf outline to make a template.

3

Working on the tissue paper and using the bradawl, make a hole in the base end of the leaf large enough to thread the silver cord through. You can make this garland as long as you like, just add one leaf approximately every 10 cm (4 in).

Christmas Tree Frames

THESE ENIGMATICALLY empty miniature picture frames with their eighteenth-century feel are so simple and satisfying to make, and look quite stunning simply displayed around the branches of your Christmas tree.

Soft copper is an enticing medium to work with. Easy to cut, it's surprisingly simple to create the lovely *repoussé* design by drawing on the back of the metal with a dry ball-point pen, thus making a raised pattern on the front which catches the light beautifully. With age copper will darken and tarnish; if you want to retain the warm glow of newly worked copper foil, polish regularly with metal polish or permanently protect it from the air with a coat of clear varnish.

When Christmas is over, use a selection of these frames to make a charming display of treasured photographs of family and friends.

MATERIALS

Roll of copper foil 0.1 mm
($4/_{1,000}$ in) thick

Small, pointed scissors

Template traced onto
tracing paper

Invisible tape

Wad of folded tissue paper

Dry ballpoint pen

Small ruler

Sewing tracing wheel

Christmas Tree Frames

1

Cut a piece of copper slightly larger than the template and stick the tracing paper design on with the tape. Rest the copper on the wad of tissue paper and transfer the design onto the metal foil beneath by drawing lightly over the guidelines with the dry ball-point pen.

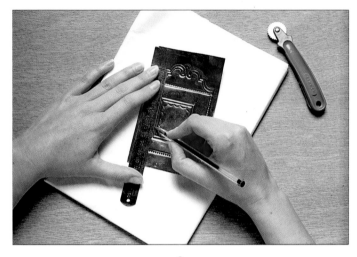

2

Remove the tracing paper and press firmly with the ball-point pen over the lightly drawn lines, using a ruler to help you draw the straight lines. Use the tracing wheel to outline the outer and inner edge of the frame as shown.

3

Draw in the latticework pattern around the frame and fill in the upper part with dots made by pressing the point of the ball-point pen very firmly into the metal. Remember that you are working on the 'wrong' side of the metal and your design will appear as a raised pattern on the other side. Carefully cut away the scalloped edge in the center and cut away the excess metal around the outside.

Trace over this outline to make a template.

CHAPTER TWO

Paper Magic

Paper is one of the most inexpensive and versatile mediums in which to work and it is now possible to find the most extraordinary variety of color and texture. The projects in this chapter explore many techniques, including folding, cutting, collage, modelling in paper pulp and papier mâché.

Papercut Garlands

INSPIRED BY THE FAMOUS Polish and Swiss papercutting traditions, these easy-to-make papercut garlands have been decorated with brightly colored feathers, sparkling sequins and ice-blue glitter. Keep them simple with a folk-art feel. Here they have been cut from crisp white paper to echo a winter theme and parade across a Christmas mantelpiece. They could also be used to decorate a kitchen shelf edge or placed along the bottom of a window to be viewed from the outside. They look especially effective displayed with snowflakes cut from a circle of similar paper neatly folded into eight sections.

For a more vibrant or seasonal feel, cut them from gold, silver or brightly colored paper, perhaps on the theme of the three kings, and display them boldly around the base of a richly decorated Christmas tree or suspend them prettily across a room.

MATERIALS

FOR THE TREE

Recycled white paper
72 x 18 cm (28½ x 7 in)

Template

Scissors

Pencil

Cutting mat

Craft knife

All-purpose clear adhesive

Selection of different sized
silver sequins

FOR THE SNOWFLAKE

White recycled paper

Dish or plate as template

Pencil

Small, pointed scissors

Christmas Tree

1

Fold the paper very carefully into 9 cm (3½ in) wide sections. It is most important at this stage to fold the paper very evenly to produce the best final results.

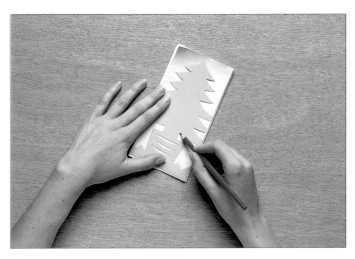

2

Trace the tree outline onto the card and neatly cut out the template. Lay the template onto the folded white paper, the base of the template against the base of the paper and draw neatly around the tree shape.

3

Remove the template and place the folded paper on the cutting mat. Cut away around the pencil lines around the tree and carefully cut away the slits in the tree tub. Remember not to cut through the edges which join the trees together. Stick a selection of the silver sequins evenly spaced up the center of the tree.

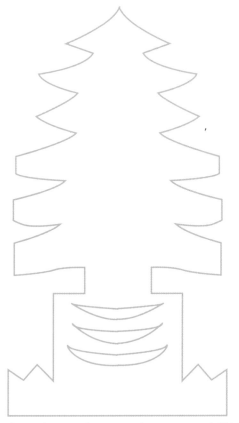

Enlarge this template on a photocopier to 150%.

Snowflake

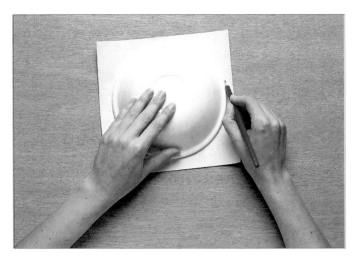

1

Using an upturned dish or plate as a template, draw neatly around the rim onto the white paper beneath. Remove the dish and cut out the circle.

2

Fold the circle in half three times, thus making eight segments. Draw the design onto the folded paper, with the cuts coming in from each folded side, making sure the design does not meet in the middle. Draw a decorative edge along the cut curved edge.

3

Using the small, pointed scissors, carefully cut out your design, making sure you do not cut through the center and separate the segments.

4

When you have finished cutting, unfold the snowflake to reveal the pretty, intricate pattern. Make a selection of these snowflakes and display them against a windowpane.

Starbursts

ALMOST MINIMAL in both their technique and their finished look, these stunning metallic foil starbursts would look perfect in a contemporary setting, with a large gold one on a clean white wall behind a Christmas dining table, or perhaps a varied group of three or four colored ones displayed against a plain, colored background. The effect is so powerful that no other decorations are necessary.

Metallic foil paper can be found in the most beautiful colors in most good art shops and usually comes in a roll. This is ideal for this project as you need a long length to fold concertina-style. The shiny surface of the paper is rather delicate and marks easily, so care should be taken when working. To make a star with points, before opening up the fan, cut the outside edges to a point.

MATERIALS

Selection of metallic foil papers
in rolls

Large scissors

Ruler

Needle

Invisible thread

Double-sided tape

Starbursts

1

Cut a length of paper 94 cm (36 in) long and 11 cm (4½ in) wide. Fold up concertina style, making each fold 2 cm (¾ in) wide. It is worth taking care at this stage to make sure the folds are as even as possible as this ensures a much better final result.

2

When the whole length has been folded, hold the paper tightly at one end as if you are holding a closed fan. Thread the needle with invisible thread and push through all the thicknesses. Tie the ends of the thread together loosely.

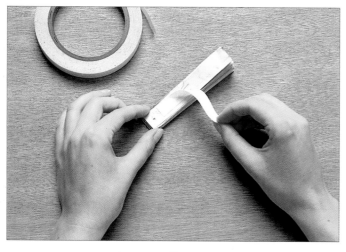

3

Lay the end of the knot along the final fold of the fan and on the wrong side of the metallic paper. Place a strip of double-sided tape along the fold, securing the knot beneath it. Remove the protective layer of the tape.

4

Open out the fan into a circle and press both ends together very carefully so they are stuck firmly together with the double-sided tape. If you want to hang the starburst, insert a length of invisible thread into the join at this stage.

Christmas Gift Tags

I T IS EXTREMELY REWARDING to make your own gift tags at Christmas and it is quite possible to create beautiful examples with the smallest scraps of paper leftover from other projects. Success depends on combining materials with contrasting colors and interesting patterns. Brightly colored papercut designs, most often of birds and elements from nature, are highly popular in Polish peasant art. You may also like to illustrate the theme from a traditional Christmas carol, such as 'The Twelve Days of Christmas' or 'I Saw Three Ships Come Sailing By'.

The tags shown here are decorated with scraps of origami paper, richly dyed hand-made paper, and pieces cut from Chinese New Year 'money' – small sheets of paper decorated in vibrant red and gold and available from Chinese supermarkets.

MATERIALS

Colored origami paper

Templates

Pencil

Small scissors

Scraps of colored hand-made thick paper

Paper glue

Chinese New Year 'money'

Pinking shears

Hole punch

Short lengths of narrow ribbon

Christmas Gift Tags

1

Draw around the bird template on a piece of pink origami paper and cut out. Cut out a background slightly larger than the bird from colored hand-made paper. Stick the bird into the center with the paper glue and cut out freehand a crown and wings from the gold part of the Chinese 'money'. Stick in place.

2

Now cut a strip of the same paper the width of the card and trim the top edge with the pinking shears. Stick this along the bottom so it just covers the bird's feet.

3

Cut around the whole tag with pinking shears, keeping the bird centrally placed. Make a hole in one corner with the hole punch and thread with a pretty ribbon.

Fold line

Enlarge the bird templates on a photocopier to 145%. Use the tree template at this size, folding the origami paper in half to create a symmetrical tree.

Christmas Wrapping Paper

THE TRADITIONAL TECHNIQUE of paste painting, where paint is mixed with wallpaper paste to a slimy consistency to slow down the drying time and thus make it easier to work designs, has been used to produce these richly decorated papers. It is an ancient technique and was often used to make endpapers in the craft of bookbinding. It would also make a lovely cover for a book or small portfolio. If you are really feeling ambitious, you could attempt to wallpaper a whole room using this technique.

Be prepared to work at speed to complete the papers — you need to complete the design before the paint starts to dry. Working quickly often produces a freedom of approach which is reflected in a more fluid design.

MATERIALS

FOR THE STRIPED PAPER

Fungicide-free wallpaper paste

Pale blue cartridge paper

Purple acrylic paint

Dark blue acrylic paint

Two dishes for paint

Newspaper

Large paintbrush

Rubber decorator's combs, each about 3 cm (1¼ in) wide, one with a flat edge and one with serrated teeth

FOR THE SNOWFLAKE PAPER

Small circles of origami paper

Small, pointed scissors

Sheets of ready-made Christmas wrapping paper speckled with gold

Spray glue

Large paintbrush

Dark blue paint mixed with wallpaper paste

Craft knife

Striped Paper

1

Mix the wallpaper paste with water and stir until it has a fairly runny consistency. Mix together with the paint, adding a little more water if necessary, and pour into dishes. Lay the cartridge paper on the newspaper and paint three large blue stripes along the length of the paper.

2

Add two thick stripes with the purple paint, using large sweeping strokes and blending lightly at the joins with the stripes of blue paint.

3

Working quickly before the paint begins to dry, wiggle the serrated rubber comb swiftly along the overlap where the two colours meet.

4

Using the flat-edged piece of rubber, wiggle the edge of the end of this between the combed lines to create a wavy line, then set aside to dry.

Snowflake Paper

1

Fold a circle of origami paper into segments and cut out a snowflake design. For one sheet of wrapping paper you will need to cut out twelve different designs; they can, however, be used more than once.

2

Lightly spray the backs of the snowflakes with the spray glue and lay them evenly spaced, as shown, on the gold speckled background paper. Press them firmly with the palm of your hand to make sure they are well adhered to the paper below.

3

Dip the large brush into the ready-mixed blue paint and using broad sweeps, paint all over the surface quickly. The paint should be thin enough to reveal the water-resistant gold speckles beneath.

4

As soon as you have finished painting, gently push the tip of the craft knife under the edge of a snowflake and lift off. Repeat until all have been removed. Set the paper aside to dry.

Miniature Papier Mâché Houses

THESE BRIGHT AND COLORFUL little houses were inspired by the old Polish custom of making Christmas cribs in the form of houses, churches and amazing palaces. They were made from card, wrapped in paper and were highly decorated with glittery foils. Groups of carollers carried the largest examples around the villages at Christmas. The tradition still continues to this day and many towns hold competitions to judge the best crib.

The versions shown here could be displayed in a row like a village street or balanced on the branches of a Christmas tree.

There are two main methods of working with papier mâché – using paper pulp (as on page 58) or pasting layers of paper over a base of thin cardboard (as shown here). This method is dries more quickly and, with a coat of gesso as a priming layer, becomes very strong, lending itself well to these bold and colorful decorations.

MATERIALS

Thin cardboard

Scissors

PVA glue

Fungicide-free wallpaper paste

Recycled white paper

Acrylic gesso

Paintbrush

Acrylic paint in blue, pink, orange and yellow

Selection of silver cord, braids and ric-rac

Selection of shaped sequins

All-purpose clear adhesive

Miniature Papier Mâché Houses

1

Draw the elements of the house on to the cardboard – base, back, front, two gable ends, two roof pieces and roof ridge – and cut out. Using PVA glue, stick the front and sides to the base and to each other. Hold in place for a minute or two until the glue begins to set, then add the front and back sections of the roof, finally adding the roof ridge. Allow the glue to dry.

2

Mix the wallpaper paste and tear the paper up into small squares. Smear lightly with the paste and cover the entire house with paper, taking it under the base. Allow to dry on a radiator or in a warm place for an hour.

3

Paint the house with two coats of acrylic gesso, allowing it to dry thoroughly between each coat.

4

Mix the blue acrylic paint on a saucer and paint each gable end – you may need to apply two coats for even coverage.

5

Paint the front and back pink, the base and roof orange and the roof ridge yellow. Always clean the brush very thoroughly between each different color to keep the colors bright.

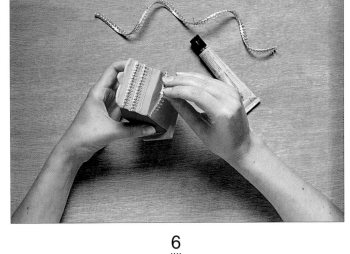

6

Put three strips of the clear glue along the front of the roof and stick some of the decorative braid in place. Repeat on the back of the roof.

7

Add the silver ric-rac to the front and back and stick the cord around all the edges of the base, house and roof. Dissect the blue gable ends with a length of cord that passes over the roof and down the other side.

8

Lastly, add the sequin decoration, large blue stars at the front and back, and smaller sequins along the roof ridge. Cut the leaves in half and arrange on either side of the silver cord on the gable ends, and finish off with two pink flowers.

Christmas Cards

Mᴵᴸᴸᴵᴼⁿˢ OF commercially printed cards are sent each Christmas and it is quite possible to receive a number of duplicate designs, so it is always a special surprise to receive a personal hand-made Christmas card.

These lovely examples using simple plain background colors overlaid with the lustrous metallic paper crowns are no exception. The crowns have been cleverly decorated on the wrong side using a simple sewing tracing wheel. Once you have mastered the crown theme, try inventing your own images and decorate them in the same way.

To make them really stand out from the moment they arrive through the letterbox, make your own matching envelopes. Simply unstick an appropriate sized envelope and use it as a template for cutting a new one from a brightly colored piece of paper (make sure the paper is thick enough to withstand the postal system!).

MATERIALS

Metallic foil papers

Crown template

Pencil

Scissors

Wad of folded tissue paper

Sewing tracing wheel

Red card 30 x 20 cm
(12 x 8 in)

Colored origami paper
10 x 15 cm (4 x 6 in)

Spray glue

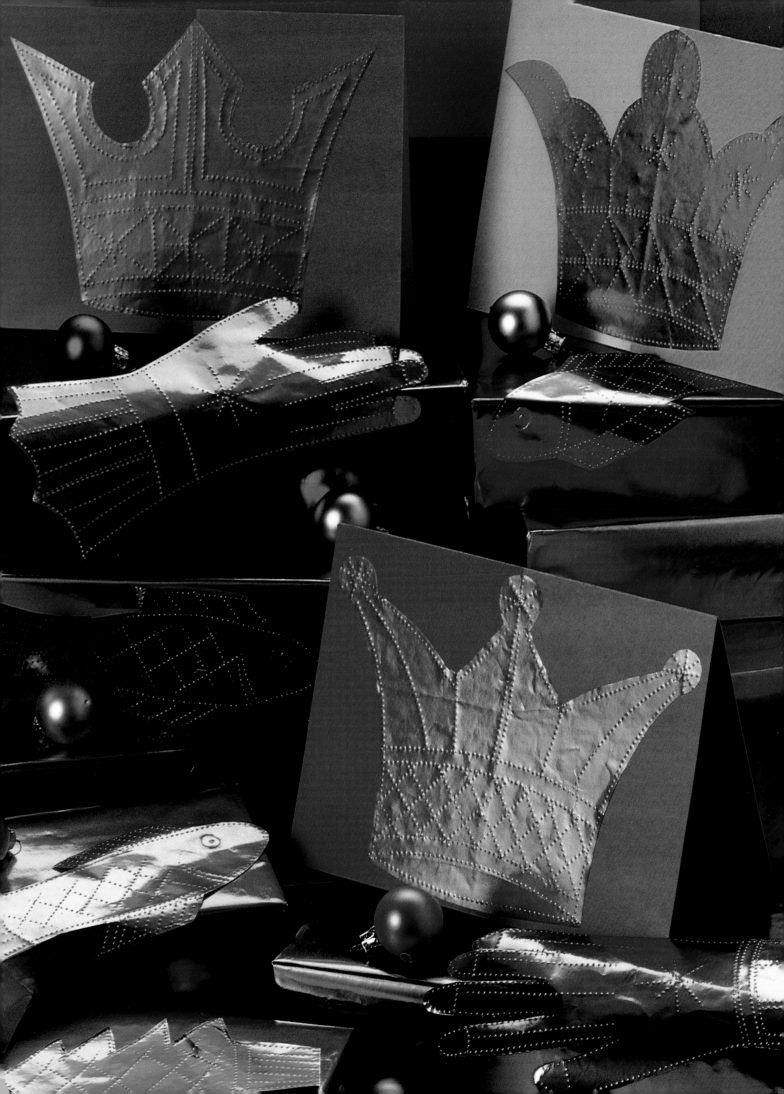

Christmas Cards

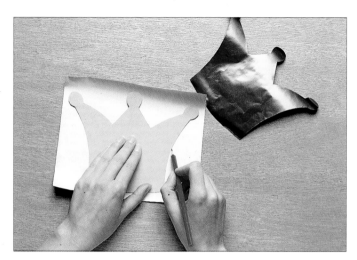

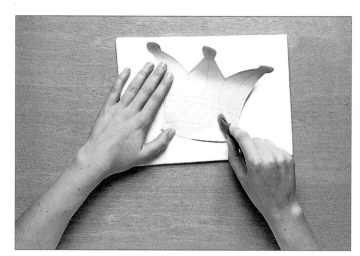

1
....

Cut out a piece of the metallic foil paper (handle it very carefully as it marks easily) and place the crown template onto the wrong side. Draw round it neatly with the pencil and cut out.

2
....

Still working on the back, mark the design on the foil paper with a pencil. Place the foil paper on the wad of folded tissue paper and roll the tracing wheel over the pencil guidelines. This will appear on the metallic side as raised dotted lines which catch the light beautifully.

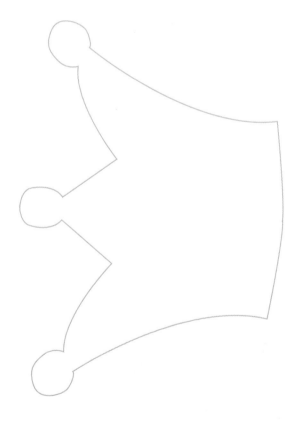

Enlarge this template on a photocopier to 215%.

3
....

Fold the red card carefully in half scoring along the fold line and, using the spray glue, stick the red and orange origami paper very neatly in place, butting up to each other in the centre of the card. Finally, spray the back of the crown design and stick centrally over the two-tone background.

Star-shaped Candle Holders

PAPIER MÂCHÉ translated from the French means chewed paper. It is an infinitely adaptable medium which is inexpensive, lightweight, easy to handle and requires no special skills or equipment. It has the advantage of being able to imitate other materials such as wood, clay or stone. Papier mâché responds to decorative finishes very well and looks particularly beautiful when gilded.

It has a long history which reached a fashionable peak in Europe and America in the second half of the nineteenth century when it was used to make furniture and all types of decorative objects, often inlaid with mother-of-pearl. It is still widely used in folk art all over the world, most particularly in mask making. Papier mâché pulp can be bought from good craft shops.

MATERIALS

Template

Thin cardboard

Scissors

PVA glue

Nightlight with
aluminum holder

Papier mâché pulp
(proprietary brand)

Ready-made decorator's filler

Small kitchen knife

White recycled paper

Fungicide-free wallpaper paste

Acrylic gesso

2 paintbrushes

Pale blue acrylic paint

Silver gilt cream

Rag, for polishing

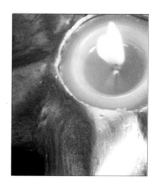

Star-shaped Candle Holders

1
....

Draw around the template on the cardboard and cut out carefully with the scissors. Place a small amount of PVA glue into the center of the cardboard shape and stick the nightlight holder in place on top. Allow to dry.

2
....

Mix the paper pulp according to the maker's instructions. Add a little ready-made decorator's filler for additional strength and to prevent shrinkage. Start to build up the pulp over the points of the star up to the level of the nightlight holder. Smooth with the kitchen knife, defining each point into two sides, and allow to dry overnight in a warm place.

3
....

Tear the paper into small squares, smear lightly with the wallpaper paste and smooth onto the star. Turn under the base. Allow to dry thoroughly.

Enlarge this template on a photocopier to 125%.

4

Paint the whole star with two coats of gesso and allow to dry. Gesso is actually a thick priming paint so ordinary acrylic primer will also suffice.

5

Next, paint the gesso-primed star with the pale blue paint. Use two coats if necessary to completely cover the holder and set aside to dry.

6

Working quickly and using a slightly stiffer brush, apply the silver gilt cream all over the surface of the star. Don't worry if some of the blue undercoat is visible.

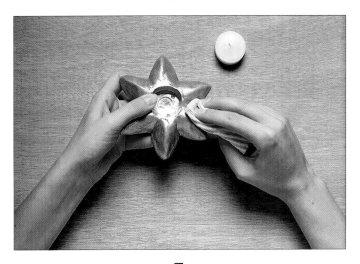

7

Wait five minutes to allow the gilt cream to dry slightly and then rub vigorously with the rag to distress the surface of the silver and reveal some of the blue undercoat. Finally, polish with a clean rag and place the nightlight in the center.

CHAPTER THREE

Natural Glories

The natural world has always been a source of inspiration for artists and craftspeople. Plan ahead for Christmas – during the warm months collect flowers, seedheads and leaves. Watch them turn papery and more subtle in color as they dry, ready for use in enchanting and unusual decorations.

Honesty Wreath

Make a welcome change from the rather over-used dark green ivy or holly and predictable red berries by creating this ethereal wintry wreath in palest green and silver to grace your front door.

This unusual and magical combination uses the papery seedheads of honesty and silver thistles which grow so abundantly in the Swiss Alps, acting like little barometers which open in dry weather and close slightly when the air becomes damp. The small honesty branches are secured simply by pushing them into the twiggy wreath base, while the thistles are fastened on with short lengths of florists' wire. The garland is then finished off beautifully with a sumptuous grey-green satin ribbon at the top.

MATERIALS

Twiggy wreath base

Large bunch of dried honesty

6 silver thistles

Bradawl

Lengths of florists' wire 35 cm
(14 in) long

1.5 m (60 in) grey satin ribbon
7 cm (2¾ in) wide

Golden Swag

1

Cut a length of organdie on the bias 2.3 m (90 in) long by 12.5 cm (5 in) wide. Cut both ends into a point, turn over a small hem and pin to hold in place. Hand stitch neatly with running stitch and remove the pins.

2

Lay the gold metallic ribbon across the fabric 10 cm (4 in) from the end, pin in the middle and stitch firmly in place across the width of the ribbon. Tie the ribbon loosely into a double knot and neaten the ends.

3

Spray the dried flowerbuds very lightly with the gold spray to give just a hint of gold. Allow to dry. Lay a flowerhead onto the background 10 cm (4 in) from the ribbon and stitch in place around the stem.

4

Continue adding ribbons and flowerbuds alternately in this manner along the whole length of the swag. Finally, sew the gold tassels in place on each of the pointed ends.

CHAPTER FOUR

Ribbons, Beads and Bows

Imagination, simple sewing skills and an interesting collection of exotic fabric scraps, feathers, silky ribbons, glittering braids, iridescent glass beads and sequins in a myriad of shapes and colors are used to make these rich and lustrous projects.

Beaded Birds

THESE EXQUISITE GLITTERY and sequinned birds are inspired by work from the Indian subcontinent where little animals made from exotic scraps of fabric festooned with tiny mirrors, beads, sequins and colorful embroidery are sewn together to hang as a vertical garland. Use up small scraps of dress-making fabric and visit a good haberdashery shop to choose braids, ribbons and trimmings. Feathers come in all colors and sizes and add a touch of exotic reality to these magical birds.

To brighten up winter, make a whole flock of these birds and settle them onto a bare branch which has been sprayed with white or silver paint.

MATERIALS

Templates of bird body
and wing (see page 126)

Scraps of purple lurex
and orange silk

Pins

Scissors

Needle

Invisible thread

Polyester stuffing

Pink star sequins for eyes

Tiny blue glass beads

Small bronze sequins

Purple feather wands

PVA glue

Selection of narrow ribbons and
gold braid

50 cm (20 in) glittery cord

Tiny metal beads

1

Pin the bird body template onto a double thickness of the orange silk and the wing template onto a double thickness of the purple lurex. Cut out.

2

Sew the body parts together by hand or preferably with a sewing machine, leaving an opening at the tail end and along the middle of the breast. Stuff loosely with the polyester wadding and sew the breast hole up neatly.

3

Pin a wing onto either side of the body and sew in place using the invisible thread, turning the lurex fabric under as you go.

4

Sew the pink sequins topped with the tiny blue glass beads onto both sides of the bird's head to make the eyes. Sew more blue beads on top of the small bronze sequins to decorate each wing.

5

Gather and twist the wire ends of the feathers into a bunch. Turn a small hem inside at the tail opening and push the tail into place. It may help to put a little PVA glue in with the tail to hold it firmly. Sew the tail opening together neatly.

6

Continue decorating the body with the bands of narrow ribbon and braid as shown. Sew the tiny metal beads between the braid. Stitch a length of glittery cord around the edge of the body to finish.

Christmas Stockings

FORGET THE LUMPY and ungracious stockings that everybody expects to see at Christmas and make these really elegant versions to hang in anticipation at the end of a bed or along the mantelpiece on Christmas Eve. Fashioned in the shape of a Victorian boot with antique crocheted, embroidered or quilted cuffs over lovely red and white woven material, these stockings make long-lasting gifts that may be passed down through generations and used year after year.

Only simple sewing skills and the ability to follow a pattern are required. For the best result, use a sewing machine, saving your hand-sewing skills for adding the decorative cuffs. The striking red snowflake design is taken from an embroidered chair cover found in an old chalet in the Swiss Alps. It is easy to find examples of interesting fabrics, lace and crochet in antique shops and markets.

MATERIALS

Pattern template on tracing paper for boot, cuff and loop (see page 126)

Woven red and white fabric

Plain lining

Pins

Scissors

Needle

Thread

Antique crochet

90

Christmas Stockings

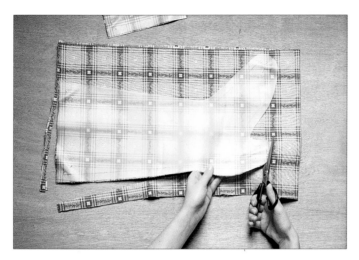

1

Pin the traced pattern onto a double thickness of fabric and cut out. Cut the hanging loop from the red and white fabric and cut two thicknesses of lining.

2

Pin the two stockings together, right sides facing. Using the sewing machine, sew the stockings together, leaving them open at the top. Do the same with the lining. Snip the curved part of the seams so they will turn inside out easily without pulling.

3

Press the seams open on both the lining and the stocking. Turn over a small hem onto the wrong side of the fabric and pin in place. Do the same with the lining and press with a hot iron.

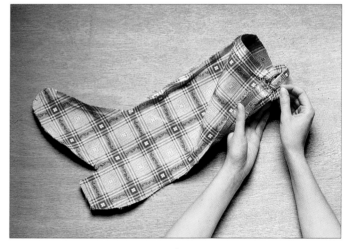

4

Fold the hanging loop in half lengthways, right sides facing. Sew along the long edge and then turn the tube inside out. Press and pin in place on either side of the back seam of the stocking.

5

Turn the stocking the right side out and slip the lining inside it, fitting the heels and toes together. Pin together at the top. Neatly stitch the boot, loop and lining together.

6

Pin the crochet border around the top of the boot and neatly stitch in place.

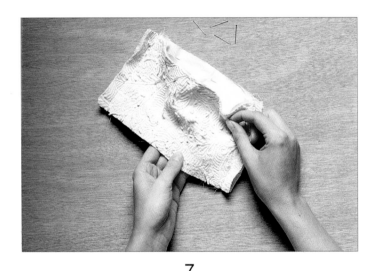

7

To make a boot with a quilted or fabric cuff, use the cuff pattern to cut out two thicknesses of the fabric for the cuff. Cut two linings as well. With the right side of the fabric facing the lining, sew up the two side seams of the lining and cuff fabric. Press the seams open.

8

Turn right side out and slip the cuff inside boot. Pin to the top of the boot and stitch in place, enclosing the hanging loop. Pull out the cuff and turn it over the top of the stocking. Press with a hot iron.

Glittery Net Hearts

THESE ORIGINAL and adaptable little tree decorations are so simple and inexpensive to make from scraps of colored net, sequins and saved sweet wrappers. They are light and flexible and can be easily tucked into the branches of your Christmas tree.

The principle of sewing objects in-between two transparent layers could be applied in many different ways – tiny shells between sheets of iridescent cellophane, miniature jewels enclosed in metallic organdie, dried and pressed flowers sandwiched between the finest muslin, or perhaps tiny nuts and seeds held between translucent Japanese paper and displayed against the light to reveal the contents.

MATERIALS

Card for template

Scissors

Scraps of colored net

Collection of glittery sweet wrappers

Pink, red and silver sequins

Pins

Needle

Invisible thread

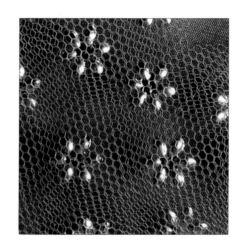

Glittery Net Hearts

1

Draw a heart on the card and cut out the template. Pin the heart template onto a double thickness of net and neatly cut around.

2

Cut the glittery sweet papers into small squares, selecting colors of a similar tonal range.

3

Carefully insert six little squares between the two layers of net, pinning through the net (not the paper) to hold each one in place. The sequins are positioned in the same way.

4

Using the invisible thread, sew around each square or sequin, carefully enclosing it between the two net layers. Remove the pins as you sew.

Beaded Spheres

THIS REMARKABLY uncomplicated project produces spectacular results, resembling the extraordinary jewel-like seeds of the exotic pomegranate. Austrian cut-glass beads combined with a matching beautiful shot-silk chiffon ribbon create a glittering richness which will enhance your Christmas decorations.

The beads are simply pinned onto a cotton pulp ball with the steel pin heads becoming part of the overall sparkling effect. Suspend them from the branches of a candlelit tree or pile them into a pretty glass stemmed bowl as a table or mantelpiece display. If you wish to hang the spheres from the tree, it is best to make them with lighter, plastic beads. These are almost indistinguishable from the heavier, glass beads and are, of course, less expensive to buy.

MATERIALS

Faceted glass or plastic beads, 5 mm (¼ in) in diameter
Small iridescent glass beads
Long steel pins
Polystyrene or cotton pulp balls, 4.5 cm (1¾ in) in diameter
Silk chiffon ribbon

100

Beaded Spheres

1

Thread one tiny glass bead onto a pin, followed by a larger faceted one. As well as being pretty, the tiny glass bead prevents the larger one from slipping off the pin as its central hole may be bigger than the head of the pin.

2

Push the pin into the cotton pulp ball so that the beads lie tightly against the curved surface.

3

Continue pushing the bead-threaded pins into the ball. They should look evenly and tightly packed together in order to conceal as much of the white surface of the cotton ball beneath as possible. Leave a small circular space at the top in which to insert the ribbon.

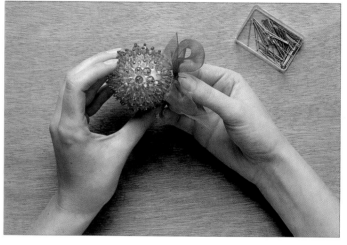

4

Tie the chiffon ribbon into a small bow, trim the ends neatly with sharp scissors and insert a pin through the center of the bow. Push the bow into the space that has been left at the top.

CHAPTER FIVE

Festive Food

Part of the excited anticipation of Christmas comes from the preparation of traditional foods in the weeks beforehand. In addition to the familiar plum pudding and Christmas cake, try the following projects which have been borrowed and interpreted from food customs around the world.

Sugarcube Castle

A STUNNING AND UNUSUAL idea for a nightlight holder, this fairytale castle is an adaptation of an American East Coast tradition. The whole castle glows white and shafts of warm light filter out from the spaces between the cubes when lit. It also has all the simplicity of traditional North African buildings with their bold and minimal design.

The art of casting in sugar can be found in several folk traditions, most notably the decorated sugar skulls and skeletons made in Mexico for the famous festival of 'The Day of The Dead', the pretty sugarcast lambs made in Poland at Easter, and the lesser known festival of 'Mouled' in Egypt where sugar horses are cast, decorated and given as presents for children to eat. This sugarcube castle, however, is stuck together with glue and, while beautiful, is definitely not edible.

MATERIALS

4 x 500 g (1 lb 1½ oz) boxes of sugarcubes

4 x 20 ml tubes of all-purpose adhesive

Ruler

Black felt pen

Sheet of paper as base

Small scraps of card for window templates

Tweezers

Nightlights and holders

Sugarcube Castle

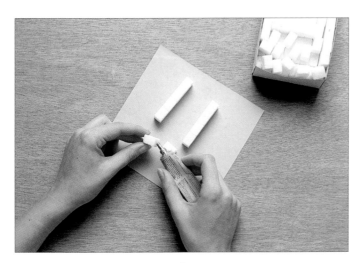

1

Make a door frame by sticking together two columns each of four sugarcubes. Stick two more cubes together and insert between the columns and stick in place. Do not use too much glue – a little goes a long way and sets quite rigid after a while

2

Draw a rectangle 26 x 12 cm (10½ x 5 in) on the base paper using the ruler and felt pen. This is an important step as it acts as the template for keeping the building firm and straight.

3

Put the ready-made door frame in the middle of the long side, stick a cube on either side of the doorway and lay the first row of sugar cubes along the black line leaving a small space between each cube, except at the corners. When you come to build the second row of cubes, use the glue to fix them in place with the centre of the top cube straddling the two cubes below.

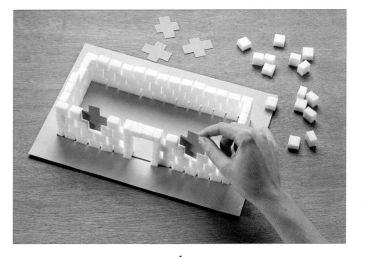

4

Make the window templates from the card by laying four cubes together to make a vertical cross. Draw around and cut out. Insert these templates into the third row on either side of the front door and two cubes away.

5

Continue building up the rows, working around the window templates. Insert the second row of window templates in the seventh row. Make the castellations as shown in the ninth row around the back and sides but continue building the front, creating three gables, one above each window.

6

Allow the glue to dry for two hours and then remove the templates carefully with tweezers. The window spaces will now be rigid and secure with no fear of collapse.

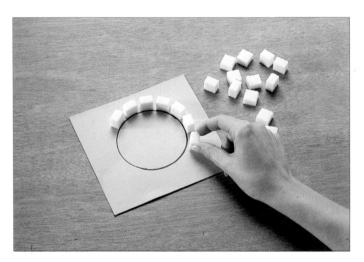

7

To make the tower, use a bowl as a template and draw around it on a piece of paper, making a circle with a diameter of approximately 9 cm (3½ in). Arrange the foundation row with cubes evenly spaced around this circle.

8

Build up nine rows, then make the castellations on the tenth row by leaving out alternate sugarcubes. After leaving to set overnight your castle is now ready to assemble by placing a tower on either side of the main building. To light the castle, put nightlights inside glass jars and place inside the buildings.

Aniseed Biscuits

ANISEED BISCUITS ARE traditionally baked at Christmas in Switzerland and Germany, where exquisite examples can be bought from good bakers' shops. They are often given as presents and, rather than being eaten, are hung on the wall as decorations.

This intriguing recipe, which rather surprisingly contains no fat, has been passed down through generations. The biscuits take many forms but by far the most enticing ones are those made using antique moulds. The ones used here are facsimiles from the Bern Historical Museum in Switzerland, using images from village life.

The addition of real aniseed to the recipe adds an exotic spice so apt for the Christmas table. The secret of successful biscuits is to beat the eggs and sugar well before adding the flour and to leave the biscuits to dry overnight before baking.

INGREDIENTS

4 eggs

500 g (1 lb 1½ oz) icing sugar

500 g (1 lb 1½ oz) white flour

20 ml (2 dessertspoons) aniseed

EQUIPMENT

Baking tray

Rolling pin

Biscuit moulds

Sharp knife

Aniseed Biscuits

1

Beat the eggs together with the icing sugar until light and fluffy, using an electric whisk if you have one. Mix in the flour and gradually add the aniseed. Turn out the mixture onto a lightly floured surface and knead very lightly. Roll out the dough evenly to a thickness of approximately 1 cm (½ in).

2

Lay the mould gently on the dough and, without pressing, cut around the mould to release a piece of dough the same size as the mould.

3

Press the mould firmly and evenly down onto the dough to transfer the image. Lift off carefully and place the biscuit on a very lightly greased baking tray.

4

Using the larger composite mould, press firmly and evenly onto the pastry. Remove the mould and cut the resulting images up into smaller biscuits. Place these on the lightly greased baking tray and, most importantly, leave to dry overnight. Bake low down in an oven preheated to 140°C/275°F/gas 1 for approximately 35 minutes or until biscuits have risen and formed a base and top layer.

Gingerbread House

THIS IS AN ELEGANT adaptation of the more homely German tradition of making a *Lebkuchen Haus* at Christmas. These confectionery masterpieces were generally more in the style of a Hansel and Gretel-type cottage, freely decorated with drifts of icing snow and lavishly adorned with brightly coloured sweets and enticing biscuits.

INGREDIENTS

100 g (4 oz) butter
200 g (7 oz) black treacle
175 g (6 oz) honey
500 g (1 lb 1½ oz) plain white flour
100 g (4 oz) ground almonds
15 ml (1 tbsp) ground ginger
5 ml (1 tsp) mixed spice
5 ml (1 tsp) cinnamon
2.5 ml (½ tsp) nutmeg
10 ml (2 tsp) bicarbonate of soda
100 g (4 oz) chopped preserved ginger
100 g (4 oz) chopped mixed peel

You will need to make 3 times this amount for the house shown here.

ROYAL ICING

500 g (1 lb 1½ oz) icing sugar
Whites of 2 large eggs
5 ml (1 tsp) lemon juice

EQUIPMENT

Rolling pin
2 baking trays
Templates (see page 127)
Small kitchen knife
Piping bag and nozzles
Cake board 23 x 33 cm (9 x 13 in)

116

Gingerbread House

1
....

Warm butter, treacle and honey in a pan until blended, then cool a little. In a bowl mix together the dry ingredients, chopped ginger and peel. Add the cooled butter mixture to the dry ingredients. Mix together, turn onto a floured surface and knead lightly. Add a little milk if the dough is too dry or a little flour if too wet. Roll out onto the greased baking tray to a thickness of 1 cm (½ in).

2
....

Lay the template on the pastry and cut around it. Repeat for the sides and roof pieces. The back is cut from the front template without cutting out the windows and door. Preheat the oven to 200°C/400°F/gas 6 and bake for about 20 minutes until a rich brown colour. Allow to cool, then remove from the tray. If the gingerbread has spread, replace the template and cut around once more.

3
....

Beat the egg whites until frothy and slowly add the sifted sugar and lemon juice, beating until it holds up in peaks. Fill the icing bag and use the smallest nozzle to pipe around the windows and door. Pipe a double line around the front and fill in with dots. Pipe a border along the bottom and add dots and stars. Decorate the sides as shown.

4
....

Pipe the design onto the roof pieces – a crossed border along the top with a latticework design on the main section. To finish, pipe a dot into each diamond. The back of the house need not be decorated as it will not be seen.

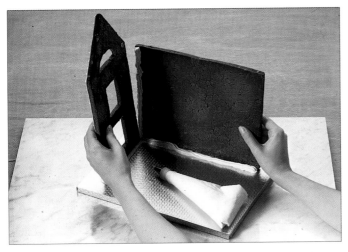

5

To make the icing glue, beat the remaining royal icing mixture until it becomes much thicker. Fill the piping bag and insert a larger nozzle. Pipe a generous amount of the icing along the side and back of the cake board. Pipe another line up the side of the back wall where it will join the side wall. Place the back and side on the icing glue and push the side against the back, making sure that they both stand upright.

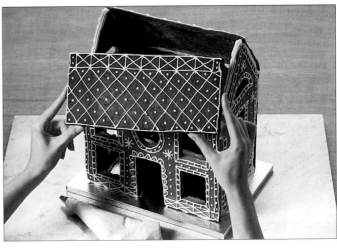

6

Continue in this manner adding the other side and front. The icing glue is very strong and should hold the pieces together well when it sets. Pipe along the top of the front and along the front edges of the gable end. Carefully place the front section of the roof on the house and press very gently into place. Repeat to attach the back section.

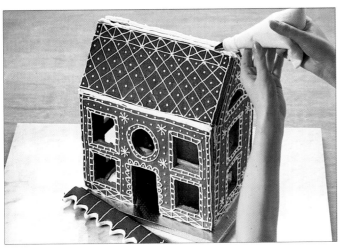

7

When the two roof sections are in place, a small gap will be left between them at the top. Pipe along both edges of this gap and fix the roof ridge in place.

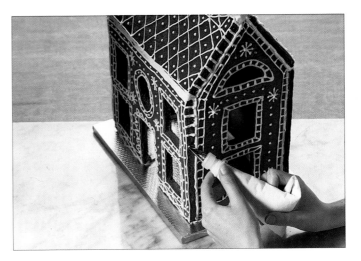

8

Clean away any icing glue that oozes out of the joins and from under the base of the house with the kitchen knife. Replace the narrow nozzle on the bag and using the original icing mixture, disguise the joins by piping over them as well as piping horizontal lines up the sides of the front and roof.

Chocolate Snowflake Stars

S IMPLE TO MAKE and decorated using the enduring wintry theme of snowflakes, these delicious star-shaped biscuits will appeal to children – in fact they could be made by children who love to stamp out interesting shapes with tin biscuit cutters. These can be found in many different shapes and sizes in good kitchen supply shops.

For extra interest, omit the chocolate from some of the mixture, making a lighter coloured pastry. Pipe these paler biscuits with a rich brown icing, made by adding some cocoa powder to the royal icing. Packed into little cellophane bags, these biscuits made a wonderful addition to a child's stocking.

INGREDIENTS

200 g (7 oz) dark chocolate

225 g (8 oz) butter, softened

225 g (8 oz) caster sugar

3 eggs

Pinch of salt

500 g (1 lb 1½ oz) flour

ROYAL ICING

500 g (1 lb 1½ oz) icing sugar

Whites of 2 large eggs

5 ml (1 teaspoon) lemon juice

EQUIPMENT

Rolling pin

Baking tray

Star-shaped biscuit cutter

Icing bag and nozzle

Chocolate Snowflake Stars

1

Melt the chocolate, add to the softened butter and mix. In another bowl beat the sugar and eggs together, add a pinch of salt and the flour. Stir in the chocolate mixture. Turn out onto a floured surface and knead lightly, then roll out the pastry to a thickness of 5 mm (¼ in).

2

Cut out the star shapes with the pastry cutter and place them carefully on a baking tray. Preheat the oven to 200°C/400°F/gas 6 and bake for 10 minutes. Remove from oven and allow to cool.

3

Sift the icing sugar. Beat the egg whites until just frothy and slowly add the sifted sugar and the lemon juice, beating all the time until the icing stands up in peaks. Fill the icing bag and, using the finest nozzle, pipe a star shape onto the biscuits. The icing must be just the right consistency to make good clean lines – if it is too runny it will spread; too stiff and it will not adhere to the biscuit when set.

4

Now pipe radiating lines from the simple star shape to form a snowflake. When the icing has set, store in an airtight tin.

Christmas Stocking (see pages 90-95)

Enlarge these templates on a photocopier to 195%.

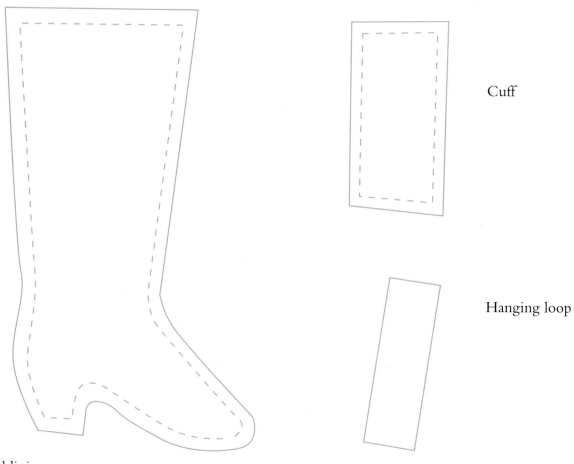

Cuff

Hanging loop

Boot and lining

Beaded Birds (see pages 86-89)

Enlarge these templates on a photocopier to 195%.

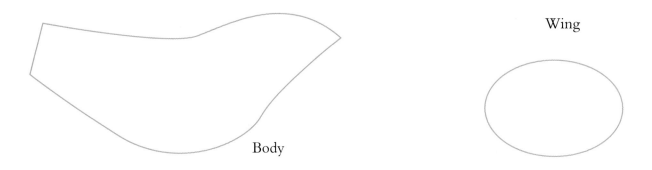

Wing

Body

Gingerbread House (see pages 116-121)

Enlarge these templates on a photocopier to 200%.

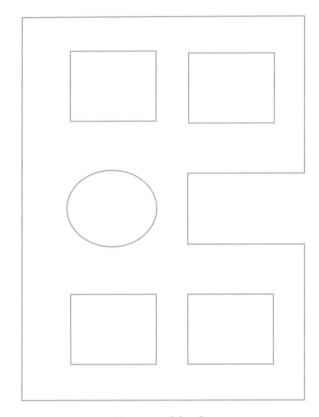

Front and back

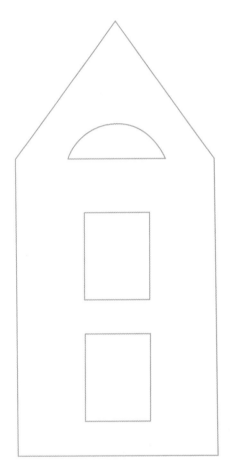

Side – use twice

Roof ridge   Roof – use twice

INDEX